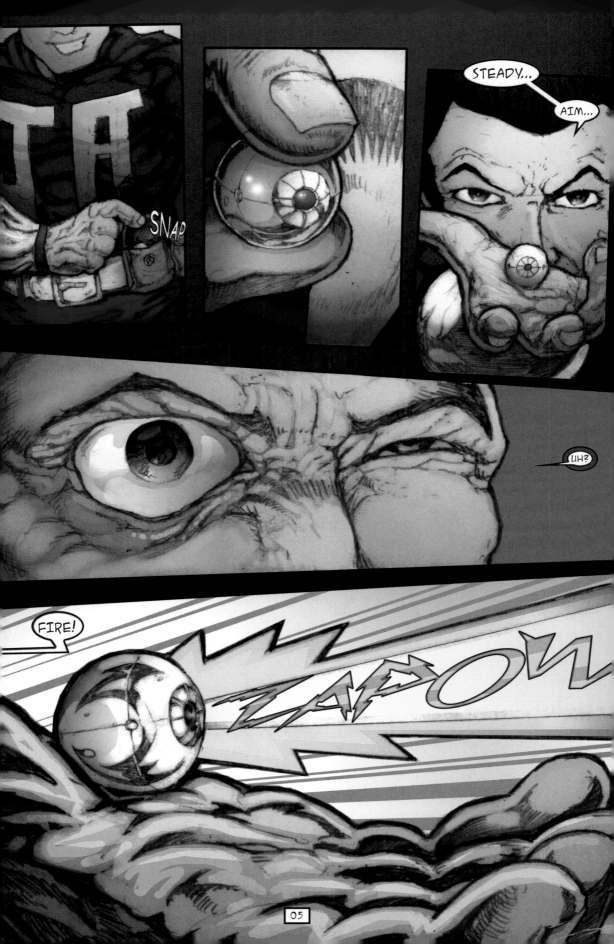

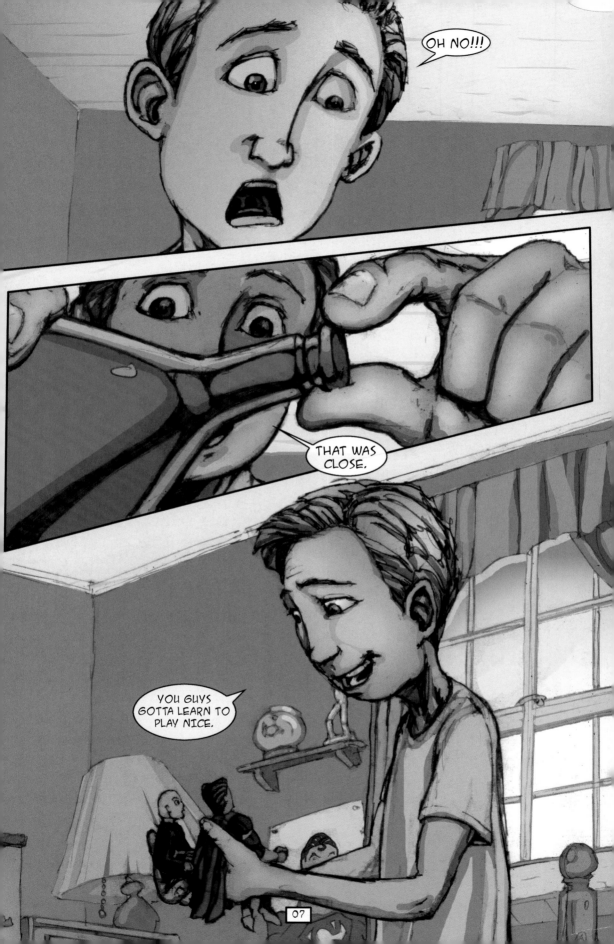

CHOW TIME BOYS.

HI, MY NAME'S ANDY.

WHEN I GROW UP I'M GONNA DRAW COMIC BOOKS...

...OR WORK AT THE SUPER CRUNCH FACTORY.

THE JUSTICE AVENGER'S MY FAVORITE SUPER HERO.

AND I LIKE BASEBALL & VIDEO GAMES.

WHATCHA READIN'?

I'M GOING OVER THE PASTOR'S MESSAGE... ...ABOUT THE FIRST KINGS OF ISRAEL.

REMEMBER SAUL & DAVID?

DAVID'S THE GUY THAT KILLED GOLIATH.

THAT'S RIGHT. HOW ABOUT SAUL? DO YOU REMEMBER HIM?

NOT REALLY.

YOU SHOULD TELL ANDY THE STORY OF DAVID.

YEAH DAD, COME ON, TELL THE STORY.

ALRIGHT...

...BUT TO REALLY TELL THE STORY I HAVE TO BEGIN WITH SAUL.

FATHER, WE HAVE SPIED ON THE PHILISTINE CAMPS.

THEIR NUMBERS?

3000 CHARIOTS, 6000 CAVALRY.

AND WHAT OF THE INFANTRY?

MORE THAN I'VE EVER SEEN.

AND HOW MANY OF OURS REMAIN?

LESS THAN HALF, FATHER.

16

PROPHET SAMUEL, WHAT SHALL WE DO? WE ONLY HAVE SIX HUNDRED MEN.

STAY STRONG SAUL.

THE ENEMY'S TROOPS ARE TOO NUMEROUS.

TRUST IN THE LORD YOUR GOD.

OUR MEN HAVE NO SWORDS.

THEY HAVE NO CHANCE.

MOST HAVE FLED TO HIDE IN THE HILLS.

SAUL, YOU ARE KING. DO NOT BE AFRAID!

THE LORD HAS PROVIDED A WAY FOR HIS PEOPLE TO...

..TRIUMPH OVER THE PHILISTINES.

TOMORROW, WE SHALL WIN THIS FIGHT.

Without telling Saul, Jonathan and his armor bearer went up to the Philistine outpost on the cliffs of Bozen. From the pass they could see the Philistines.

WE WILL LET THE PHILISTINES SEE US.

IF THEY SAY, "WE'LL COME TO YOU" THEN WE WILL STAY HERE...

...BUT IF THEY SAY, "COME UP TO US" THAT WILL BE A SIGN FROM GOD THAT WE WILL DEFEAT THEM.

LOOK! THE HEBREWS ARE COMING OUT OF THEIR HIDING PLACES!

WE HAVE NO CAUSE TO HIDE FROM YOU PHILISTINE DOGS!

COME UP TO US SO YOU MAY DIE!

LET'S GET 'EM!

19

LOOK, OVER THERE.

WE'RE BEING ATTACKED!

Then the ground quaked...

RUMBLE

...and panic struck the entire army of Philistines...

...those in the camps...

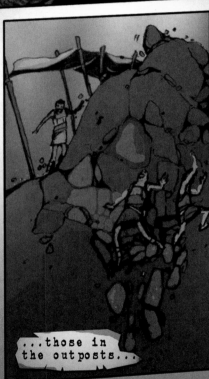

...those in the outposts...

...and those in the raiding parties.

Jonathan and the armor bearer marveled, for it was a panic sent by God.

GOD IS WITH US TODAY, JONATHAN.

INDEED HE IS.

MY FATHER MUST SEE IT THIS TIME.

...the Lord rescued the people of Israel, and the Philistines were scattered and those remaining were driven back beyond the land of Beth Aven.

WERE ALL THOSE PEOPLE KILLED?

YES, MOST OF THEM WERE.

WHY DID GOD ALLOW THAT TO HAPPEN?

THAT'S NOT THE EASIEST QUESTION TO ANSWER, ALL OF THIS HAD BEEN A LONG TIME COMING.

THE ISRAELITES HAD FOLLOWED THE LORD INTO THE PROMISED LAND, BUT MANY TIMES THEY WERE NOT AS FAITHFUL TO GOD AS THEY SHOULD HAVE BEEN.

OFTEN THE ISRAELITES REFUSED TO OBEY GOD AND TURNED FROM HIM TO WORSHIP FALSE GODS CALLED IDOLS.

BECAUSE OF THE SINS OF ISRAEL, GOD BROUGHT THEM HARDSHIPS. THE PHILISTINES CAME INTO THE LAND TO BE A TEST TO ISRAEL. THE PHILISTINES WERE POWERFUL & WAR-LIKE. THEY ALSO WORSHIPED IDOLS, WHICH THE LORD DESPISED.

AND YET, THERE WAS THE LONGSTANDING PROPHECY THAT THE ISRAELITES WERE TO POSSESS THAT LAND.

AT THE TIME OF THIS BATTLE THE PHILISTINES WERE A PEOPLE WITH WEAPONS AND RESOURCES THAT ISRAEL DID NOT HAVE, BUT BECAUSE THE LORD HAD MADE HIS COVENANT WITH THE NATION OF ISRAEL AND BECAUSE HE LOVED THEM...

...HE MADE A WAY FOR ISRAEL TO OVERCOME THE MIGHTY PHILISTINES SO THAT HE WOULD BE HELD UP AS THE ONE TRUE GOD.

UNDERSTAND?

YEAH, I THINK SO.

YOU WANT ME TO CONTINUE?

UH-HUH.

26

Looking out...

...Jonathan saw...

...the men were faint.

MY FATHER HAS PLACED THIS EXTRA BURDEN ON US TODAY.

WOULDN'T THE VICTORY BE GREATER IF WE WERE ABLE TO PARTAKE IN THE SPOILS?

That evening after the fighting was done the men rushed to eat the meat even though it had not yet been prepared according to their religious law.

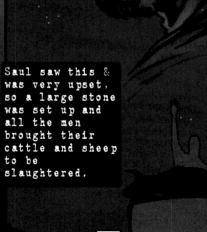

Saul saw this & was very upset, so a large stone was set up and all the men brought their cattle and sheep to be slaughtered.

And so the soldiers did not eat for a long time. When all the men had eaten Saul built an alter to the Lord and gathered the leaders together...

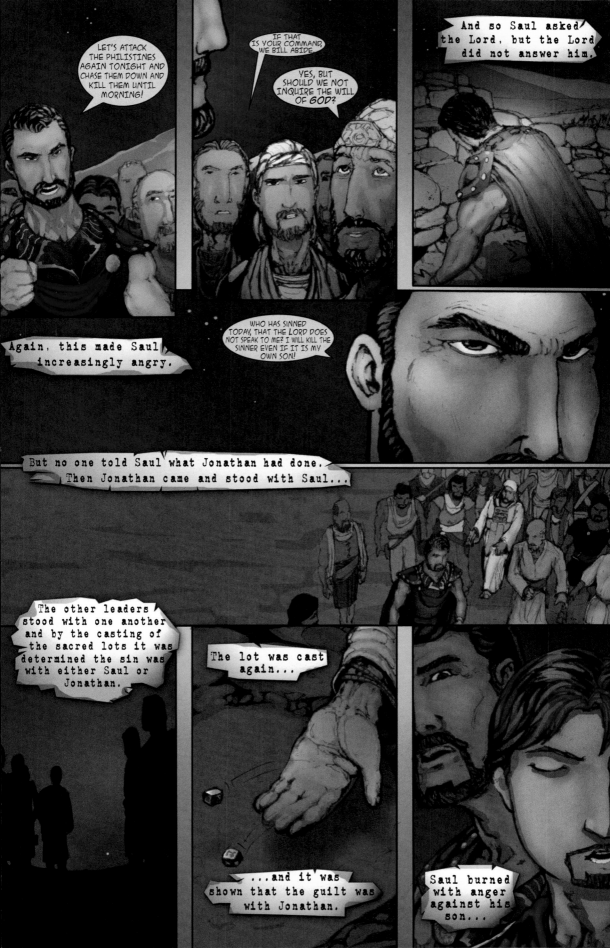

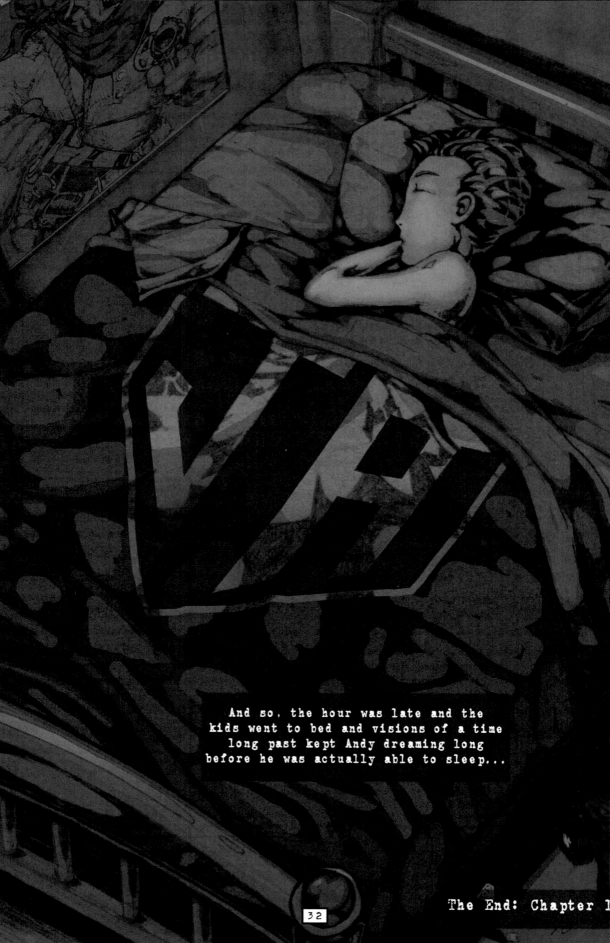

And so, the hour was late and the kids went to bed and visions of a time long past kept Andy dreaming long before he was actually able to sleep...

The End: Chapter

HAHAHA
I HAVE IT AT LAST!
The kingdom of Israel has run out of money. But Saul has built a time machine to catapult himself into the future!!!
I WILL TRAVEL 4000 YEARS INTO THE FUTURE.
THERE I WILL STEAL ENOUGH MONEY TO SAVE MY EMPIRE!

WWW.oldt

www.

I
LOVE
IT!

HE'S RIGHT HERE.

I'M GOING TO PUT HIM ON THE OTHER PHONE SO WE CAN BOTH LISTEN...

OKEY-DOKEY.

HEY DAD.

WELL ANDY, DO YOU REMEMBER WHERE WE LEFT OFF?

SAUL, THE KING, WAS UPSET THAT JONATHAN ATE THE HONEY...

...AND SAUL WANTED TO KILL JONATHAN, BUT THE REST OF THE GUYS STOPPED HIM.

OKAY, WELL LET ME THINK A BIT HERE...

...SAUL WAS MAD...

...JONATHAN WAS RESCUED...

...HERE IT IS...

"...BUT THE PEOPLE BROKE IN AND RESCUED JONATHAN SAYING, 'GOD HAS USED JONATHAN TO DEFEAT THE PHILISTINES AND DELIVER ISRAEL...'"

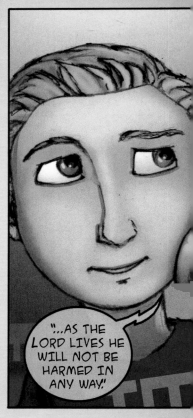

"...AS THE LORD LIVES HE WILL NOT BE HARMED IN ANY WAY."

"...SO, AT THAT TIME SAUL ABANDONED HIS PURSUIT OF THE PHILISTINES AND THE ISRAELITES RETURNED TO THEIR OWN LANDS..."

48

...Upon his return Saul was greeted at the palace gates by his family...

IT IS GOOD TO BE HOME.

WE'RE SO GLAD TO SEE YOU RETURN.

WE HEARD REPORTS THAT YOU WERE BADLY OUT-NUMBERED.

WHERE IS JONATHAN?

HE WILL RETURN SOON.

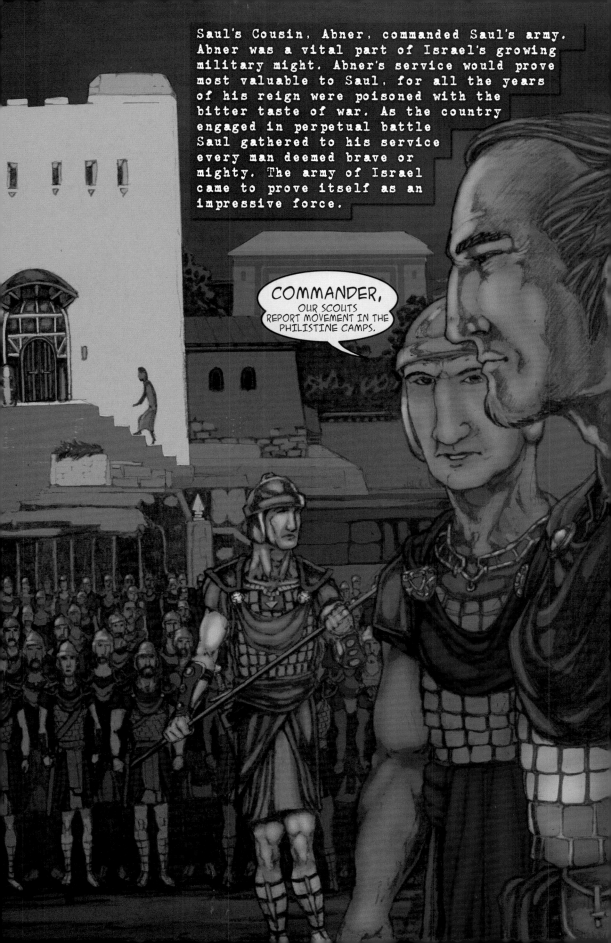

And a time came when the prophet Samuel received a message from God to give to the king.

MY LORD, SAMUEL HAS ENTERED THE PALACE.

HE REQUESTS A CONFERENCE WITH YOU. SHALL I SHOW HIM IN?

YES.. ...OF COURSE. SEND HIM IN.

HERE, PLEASE HAVE A SEAT AND EXCUSE THE MESS. IT'S BEEN A BUSY TIME.

TOO BUSY, NO?

YES, YOU'RE RIGHT... ...BUT THEN AGAIN, YOU'RE ALWAYS RIGHT...

...LIKE IN MIGRON. YOU SAID WE WOULD HAVE VICTORY.

I DIDN'T BELIEVE YOU.

WELL THEN SAUL, BELIEVE ME NOW, FOR I COME TO YOU TO DISCUSS A MATTER OF GREAT IMPORTANCE.

I'M LISTENING.

LAST NIGHT A MESSAGE CAME TO ME FROM THE LORD GOD. THE TIME HAS COME TO FULFILL THE PROMISE THAT WAS GIVEN TO OUR ANCESTOR, MOSES.

IN A TIME LONG PAST GOD SPOKE TO MOSES SAYING, "RECORD THIS ON A SCROLL...

...THAT THE NAME AMALEK WILL ONE DAY BE UTTERLY WIPED OUT FROM BENEATH THE SUN."

IN THE HISTORY OF OUR PEOPLE, SINCE OUR FREEDOM FROM SLAVERY IN EGYPT, THE AMALEKITES HAVE BEEN OUR ADVERSARIES.

I BRING TO YOU NOW A MESSAGE OF THE UTMOST SIGNIFICANCE TO YOUR THRONE.

I SAY TO YOU, AS THE ONE FIRST SENT TO ANOINT YOU AS KING, THAT THIS IS A MESSAGE FROM ALMIGHTY GOD.

HE SAYS, "I CALL YOU TO PUNISH THE AMALEKITES FOR THEIR GRIEVOUS OFFENSES AGAINST THE PEOPLE OF ISRAEL.

YOU SHALL ATTACK THE AMALEKITES SPARING NONE AND DESTROY ALL THAT IS THEIRS!"

THUS SPEAKS THE LORD OUR GOD.

THEN IT MUST BE DONE.

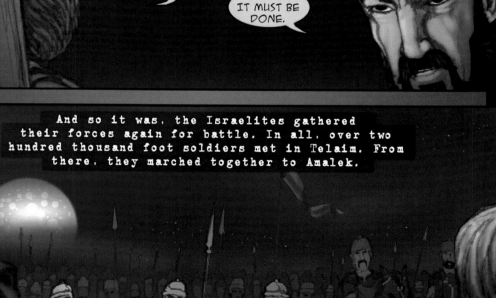

And so it was, the Israelites gathered their forces again for battle. In all, over two hundred thousand foot soldiers met in Telaim. From there, they marched together to Amalek.

COME ON YOU STUPID ANIMAL!

WHAT'S GOTTEN INTO YOU?

WHAT IS THAT SOUND?

GOD IN HEAVEN!

IT'S A GREAT ARMY.

HEYAHHH!

BURRK

LOOK! ON THE HILL!

RIDERS, STOP HIM!

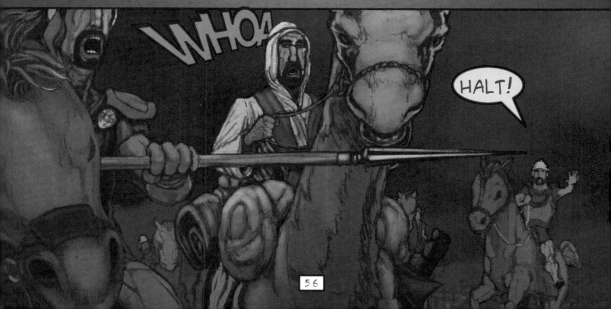

WHAT HAS HAPPENED?

In the night God spoke to Samuel saying, IT GRIEVES ME THAT SAUL WAS EVER MADE KING OF ISRAEL. HE HAS REBELLED AGAINST MY COMMAND AND USED HIS AUTHORITY FOOLISHLY. MY WORDS WERE SPOKEN TO HIM SAYING 'SPARE NONE,' AND HE HAS SAVED KING AGAG FOR HIS OWN PURPOSE. MY WORDS WERE SPOKEN TO HIM SAYING, 'DESTROY ALL THAT THEY HAVE.' AND HE HAS SAVED THE BEST FOR HIMSELF.

...in a land far removed from
the troubles of kings...

...and as the moon
shone down from
the heavens...

...a young man of
seemingly little importance...

...watched over
his father's sheep.

The end: Chapter 2

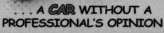

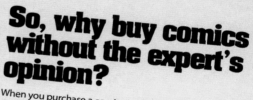

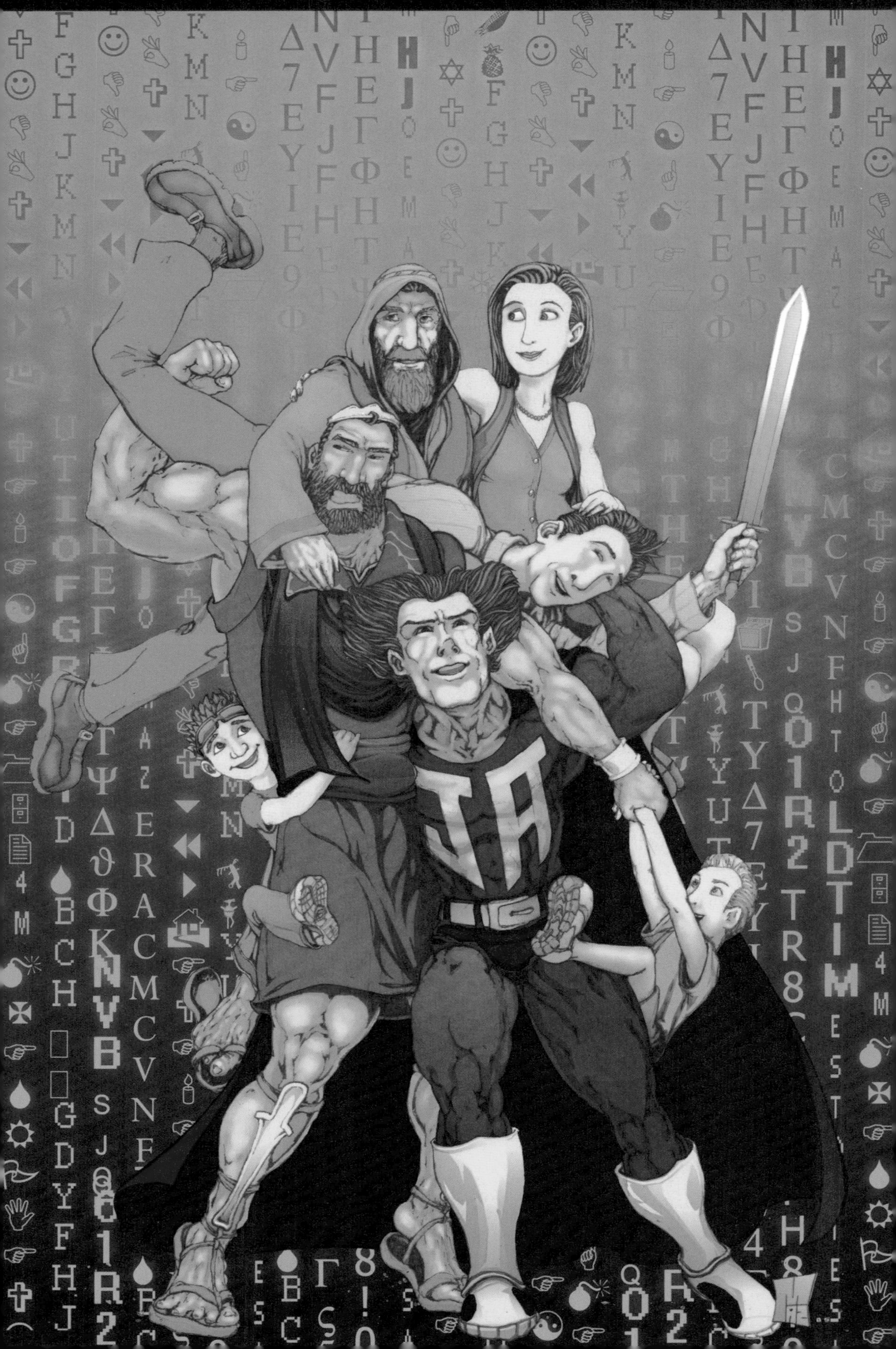

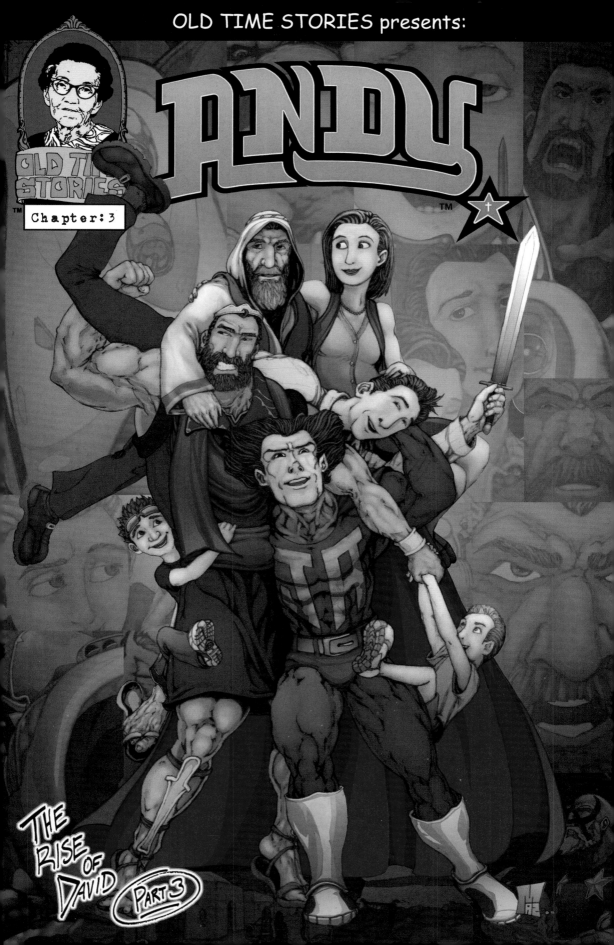

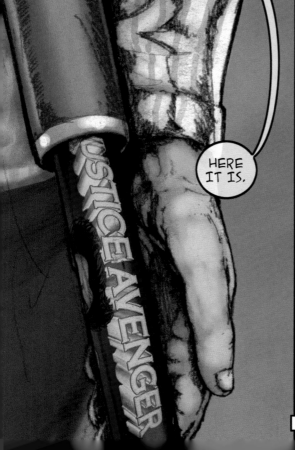

75

EXCUSE ME YOUNG MAN, I HAD EXPECTED TO FIND SAUL HERE THIS MORNING.

THE KING LEFT FOR CARMEL HOURS AGO TO ERECT A MONUMENT.

A MONUMENT TO WHAT?

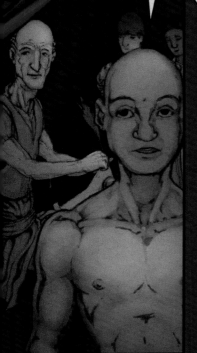

TO HIMSELF MY LORD.

FROM CARMEL HE IS GOING TO GILGAL WHERE WE WILL MEET HIM.

WE SHALL LEAVE IN A FEW HOURS IF YOU WISH TO RIDE IN OUR COMPANY.

MOST KIND OF YOU SCRIBE, BUT NO. WE MUST MAKE HASTE.

MEN, SEE TO OUR PROVISIONS.

I RODE UP BESIDE HIM AND GRABBED HIM BY THE TUNIC AND SNATCHED THE SCOUNDREL RIGHT OUT FROM BETWEEN THE CAMEL'S HUMPS!

HA HA HA

HA HA YEAH

WHAT EVER DID YOU DO, LORD?

YES, TELL US WHAT HAPPENED, LORD SAUL!

WAHOOO

HA HA HA

STAND ASIDE! STAND ASIDE! COMING THROUGH!

WAHOOO WAHOON YEAH

WAHOO

WAHOOO YEAH

MY LORD, THE PROPHET SAMUEL HAS ARRIVED! HE URGENTLY WISHES TO SPEAK WITH YOU.

HAVE HIM MEET ME IN THE PRIVATE GARDEN.

BAA MOHR BAA BAA

SAMUEL! THE AMALEKITES ARE DEFEATED. THE LORD'S COMMAND HAS BEEN FULFILLED.

THEN EXPLAIN TO ME THE SOUNDS OF SHEEP AND OXEN IN MY EARS.

CALM YOURSELF FRIEND.

THE PEOPLE HAVE SAVED THE FINEST ANIMALS TO BE SACRIFICED TO THE LORD. THE OTHER CREATURES HAVE ALREADY BEEN SLAIN.

LISTEN TO YOURSELF! DO YOU NOT HEAR YOUR OWN WORDS?

THIS IS NO GAME. YOU WERE GIVEN A COMMAND FROM ALMIGHTY GOD!

I KNOW...

THE LORD SPOKE AGAIN TO ME LAST NIGHT.

WHEN YOU SAW YOURSELF AS A MAN OF LITTLE SIGNIFICANCE, WERE YOU NOT KNOWN IN ALL THE LANDS OF ISRAEL?

AND WERE YOU NOT ANOINTED AND MADE KING OF THOSE LANDS?

YES I WAS.

THE LORD SAID TO YOU, GO AND ERADICATE THE AMALEKITES. ALL THAT IS THEIRS IS TO BE DESTROYED. ALL THEIR PEOPLE MUST BE KILLED.

AND THE TREASURES...

THEY WERE NOT DESTROYED AND THE LIVESTOCK LIVES STILL!

THEY HAVE BEEN TAKEN BY GOD'S CHOSEN PEOPLE TO BE SACRIFICED TO OUR LORD.

YOU HAVE FORSAKEN GOD AND NOW GOD HAS FORSAKEN YOU, KING.

WHAT? SAMUEL, PLEASE, NO! NOT LIKE THIS! I SEE I HAVE ERRED, BUT... I FEARED THE PEOPLE. THEY ARE DISGRUNTLED AND DO NOT FEAR ME. PLEASE, COME WITH ME TO THE TEMPLE AND PRAY FORGIVENESS OVER ME THAT I WILL FIND ATONEMENT.

YOUR TIME FOR ATONEMENT HAS PASSED.

RIP

NOOO!

AS THIS ROBE HAS TORN, SO HAS THE LORD TORN ISRAEL FROM YOU!

ISRAEL'S CROWN WILL PASS TO ANOTHER, FOR GOD IS NOT LIKE SINFUL MAN. HE DOES NOT LIE, NOR CHANGE HIS MIND.

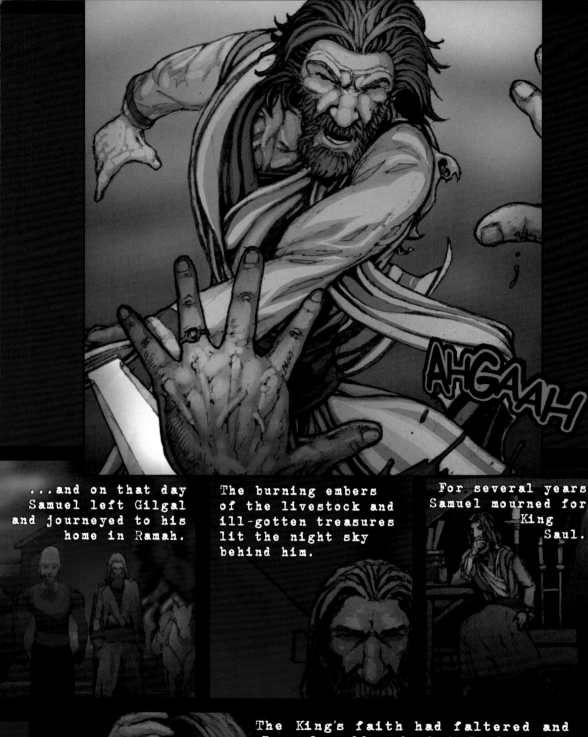

...and on that day Samuel left Gilgal and journeyed to his home in Ramah.

The burning embers of the livestock and ill-gotten treasures lit the night sky behind him.

For several years Samuel mourned for King Saul.

The King's faith had faltered and Israel suffered, but Saul would no longer look to Samuel for counsel or prayer.

As a chapter was closing in the lives of Samuel and Saul, a new chapter was beginning for a boy in Bethlehem.

Now David was the youngest of eight brothers. While his older brothers tended to their father's business or served in the Lord's army under the banners of Israel...

...David was given the job of shepherd.

It was considered a menial task, but David was the youngest.

In spite of a shepherd having very little prestige, David took great care in his work.

He cared for his father's sheep, watching them night and day.

If a sheep was hurt David would tend to the wound.

If a sheep strayed David would find it and return it safely to the fold.

Usually his time spent in the field came and went with little incident.

Most days blurred together, for one was the same as another...

...but a time came when a lion crept upon the flock.

The lion snatched up a sheep in it's terrible jaws.

But David, catching the beast by it's beard, freed the sheep.

With a club in hand, David killed the mighty animal.

So it was. And after the lion fell, David knew in his heart that The Lord had delivered him from certain death.

So David praised The Lord
and he would never forget what happened
that day...

...in a lonely field...

...to a
simple shepherd boy.

-In Ramah-

MY LORD...

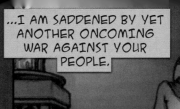

...I AM SADDENED BY YET ANOTHER ONCOMING WAR AGAINST YOUR PEOPLE.

I FEAR THAT KING SAUL, SON OF KISH, HAS LOST HIS WAY IN A SEA OF DARKNESS AND DESPAIR.

WAR TEARS AT OUR PEOPLE, LORD. COUNTLESS MOTHERS HAVE BECOME CHILDLESS...

...MANY A YOUNG MAID, NOW A WIDOW.

IN SOME PARTS EVEN THE SICK AND WEAK MUST TAKE UP ARMS.

LORD, I BEG YOU, PLEASE GRANT MERCY ON YOUR PEOPLE WHO HAVE SUFFERED SO.

BESTOW THE LIGHT OF YOUR WISDOM ON SAUL, OUR KING.

OH GOD, MY HEART BREAKS FOR HIM.

HOW AM I TO GO, LORD? IF SAUL LEARNS OF THE ANOINTING HE WILL EXECUTE ME.

SAMUEL, WHERE ARE YOU OFF TO?

TAKE WITH YOU A HEIFER AND PROCLAIM...

THIS ANIMAL IS TO BE SACRIFICED TO THE LORD IN BETHLEHEM.

WE ARE ADVISORS TO THE KING.

I AM DOEG.

AND I AM EZU.

I AM SURE IT WOULD PLEASE LORD SAUL IF WE ACCOMPANIED YOU.

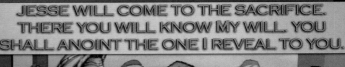

JESSE WILL COME TO THE SACRIFICE. THERE YOU WILL KNOW MY WILL. YOU SHALL ANOINT THE ONE I REVEAL TO YOU.

JESSE, WHO ARE THESE BOYS?

THESE ARE RADDAI AND OZEM, TWO OF MY SONS.

GO AND HAVE ALL YOUR SONS BROUGHT BEFORE ME,

FOR THE LORD INTENDS GREAT THINGS FROM THE ONE I SHALL ANOINT.

HOW WILL I KNOW THE ONE YOU SEEK?

YOU WILL KNOW.

The end: Chapter 3